IT'S A LONG WAY TO GUACAMOLE
*The **TEX-MEX** Cookbook*

by

Ann Worley

and

Rue Judd

Drawings by Marti Patchell

D1445082

IT'S A LONG WAY TO GUACAMOLE

WRITTEN AND PUBLISHED BY TRANSPLANTED TEXANS

Ann Worley and Rue Judd

Cover Design by Margaret Jones
of Darby Digital Communications, Alexandria, Virginia

First Printing - 1978

Fourteenth Printing - 1997

Additional copies are available for $10.95, plus $2.25 postage and handling. Virginia residents add $.49 sales tax. Send to:

J & W Tex-Mex Publications
P.O. Box 983
Arlington, VA 22216
703/538-2393

Copyright © Revised Edition 1987 by Ann Worley
Library of Congress Card No.: 87-080795
ISBN: 0-9604842-2-1

cookbook
resources.

541 Doubletree Drive
Highland Village TX 75067
(972) 317-0245

CONTENTS

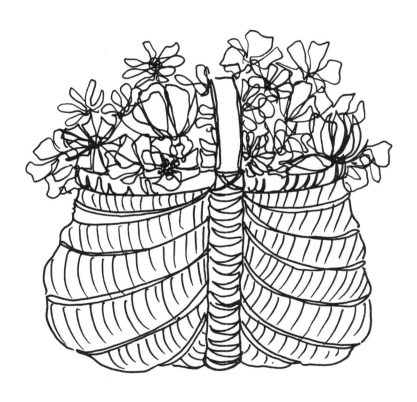

INTRODUCTION

The inspiration for *It's a Long Way to Guacamole* grew over the years as we tried to assemble a collection of the favorite, tried-and-true recipes of our fellow Tex-Mexican food aficionados in and around Washington, D.C.

A number of years ago, several Texas couples, transplanted to the Washington area, began gathering on occasional Sunday evenings for informal Mexican suppers. The hostess would plan the menu and ask each couple to bring a specific dish. Over the years the group has grown. Though some of its original members have returned to the Texas homeland, many others have arrived to take their places. Other members of the group are Texans by marriage; longing, envious Oklahomans and Louisianans; other Southwesterners; and even a few Yankees, but all enjoy TEX-MEX food.

It's a Long Way to Guacamole is a collection of recipes drawn from "the group" and our Texas families. Our Mexican food is unabashedly TEX-MEX—the food of the northern Mexican provinces which has migrated so felicitously and deliciously across the border into and throughout Texas.

There are now approximately 12 million Mexican-Americans in the United States, with increasingly wide

1

geographical distribution. Accordingly, ingredients for cooking Mexican food are available in supermarkets all over the country—not just in Texas and the Southwest—but in Washington, Boston, Atlanta, New York City, Chicago, Seattle and all points in between!

Whether you wish a simple taco and chili supper with the family, a cooperative covered-dish supper, an elegant and spicy brunch, or a festive dinner party, we hope *It's a Long Way to Guacamole* will enrich and enhance your culinary endeavors.

BASIC TECHNIQUES, INGREDIENTS, SAUCES AND FILLINGS

Mexican food originated with the Aztecs. Tortillas and tamales were being consumed with gusto long before Columbus discovered the "New World." The basics are still the same: corn, beans, chiles, tomatoes and avocados — all New World products, natural and largely unprocessed foods. The Spanish added olive oil, wheat flour, wine and some cooking variations, but these additions invariably incorporated the local ingredients. Texans have further modified this delicious food to give it its unique TEX-MEX flavor.

TORTILLAS

Tortillas (tor-tee-yas) are the thin, round, unleavened pancakes made of "masa," a coarsely ground corn flour or finely ground corn meal. Tortillas are — literally — at the bottom of TEX-MEX food — also around, in or with! The *versatile* and *essential* tortilla may be served fresh and hot from the griddle, or fried crisp, and used as an edible "plate" to be covered with other delicacies (chalupas). Tortillas are used in tacos, as a crisp wrapper, for tostados as a chip, and as a rolled pancake in enchiladas, or as a "pasta" in chilaquiles.

Tortillas are available as follows:

Canned, frozen, or pre-fried — these tortillas have been cooked but need reheating or frying to serve.

At some Mexican restaurants fresh tortillas made daily may be purchased by the dozen — telephone first!

Tortillas can be made in your kitchen — a great activity with or without children!

Freshly cooked tortillas straight from your griddle with butter and a sprinkle of salt will make you an addict! Crisp-fried tortillas from a good restaurant are hard to beat for convenience when many are needed (as for a party); however, for soft tortillas, the home-made handmade variety is by far the best.

SOFT TORTILLAS

Masa Harina by Quaker is available in most large supermarkets and always in Latin American groceries. (Caution—regular cornmeal is *not* the same and will not work!)

2 cups Masa Harina
1 cup water

Mix masa and water with a fork or your hands, blending well for a couple minutes. Dough should hold together; if not, add a little more water, a tablespoon at a time. Shape into 12 to 16 balls and cover bowl to prevent drying. Allow to stand for 15 to 20 minutes. Flatten each ball of dough with tortilla press or rolling pin to form 6 inch circles.

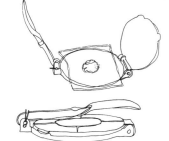

A relatively inexpensive tortilla press is available at most cookware stores, kitchen bazaars or major department stores; it makes tortilla production a total snap! Cut one plastic clear sandwich bag apart to form two squares. Place a ball of masa

dough between the plastic in the tortilla press. Press down hard with the
handle, remove the flattened dough,
gently peel away the plastic sheets, one
side at a time. Place the tortilla on an
ungreased hot griddle or iron skillet
and cook approximately one minute
on each side. Remove and place in a
dish towel or napkin to keep warm.
As one tortilla is cooking, press out
another to take its place. Children
love to pile grated cheese on the first
cooked side of the tortilla to melt
while the second side is cooking.

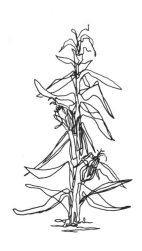

The stack of tortillas may be served immediately or kept
warm for an hour or two. If they are served after a longer
period, wrap the stack in foil and warm in a slow oven. These
soft tortillas may also be used at this point for Soft Tacos (p. 53).

TORTILLAS FOR ENCHILADAS

The fresh cooked corn tortillas (or frozen or canned variety)
are softened in oil before filling. Heat 1 inch of vegetable oil
in a 10″ skillet over medium high heat, or use deep fat fryer
set at 350°. With tongs, dip the tortilla in the oil until it becomes limp; this takes only about 5 seconds. Drain on a paper
towel, fill and roll, placing the flap side down in a casserole
(Please note: if you are using frozen tortillas, thaw 30 minutes before placing in hot oil to prevent painful splattering).

CRISP FRIED TORTILLAS

Heat 1 inch of vegetable oil, shortening, or lard in a skillet
over medium high heat (350°) or use deep fat fryer set at 350°.
Fry the whole tortilla, turning once or twice, for about a
minute until crisp. Whole crisp tortillas are also called tostados or chalupa shells.

Taco shells are made by placing the tortilla in the hot oil and then folding as soon as they soften. Hold the edges about 1 inch apart with tongs and fry until crisp. This will take about a minute per shell.

FRIED CRISP FOR CHALUPAS

TACO SHELL

To make crisp tostado chips, cut the fresh cooked tortillas (or frozen or canned variety) into quarters and fry until crisp, a handful at a time. Tostado chips are used for spooning or dipping. For a different look, cut the fresh cooked tortilla into half inch strips, using scissors. The crisp strips are good with soup instead of crackers. Serve Mexican Chicken Portuguese (p. 79) or Green Chili Stew (p. 75) over these crisp strips with rice.

BEANS

Beans are present in some form in almost every Mexican meal. In many Mexican households a pot of beans is always cooking. Beans are a valuable and inexpensive protein source and respond well to imaginative preparation. Versatile beans may be served as soon as cooked, refried, combined in sauces or used in other dishes. Pinto beans and black beans are the varieties most used in TEX-MEX cooking. Note: One cup of dried beans yields approximately 2½ cups of cooked beans. Cooked beans freeze well. Try freezing in 1½ cup quantities, using plastic sandwich bags.

CHILES

Chiles are peppers; fleshy fruits ranging from the tiny pea-sized chile pequin to the 8 inch Anaheim green chile. Not all peppers are of the eye-watering hot variety; some are sweet and mild, while others are in between. The pepper plants, es-

pecially those of the small pepper are attractive garden or
house plants. Commonly available peppers used for TEX-
MEX cooking are:

Jalapeño   Dark green; 2 to 3 inches
                  long; easy to grow in home
                  gardens; sometimes avail-
                  able fresh in large markets;
                  hot; easily available canned
                  and pickled whole or sliced

Serrano   Dark, dark green (turns red
                  as it gets very mature); ½ to
                  ¾ inch in diameter; very hot;
                  available fresh as well as
                  both canned and pickled

Green Chiles   Bright green; 5 to 6 inches
or   long and 1½ to 2 inches in
(Poblanos)   diameter at top; varies from
                  mild to hot; often available
                  fresh; always available
                  canned (labeled Whole
                  Green Chiles), use for Chiles
                  Relleños; also available
                  chopped

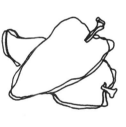

Chile Pequin   Tiny, pea sized bright dark
                  green changing to bright red;
                  extremely hot! use with cau-
                  tion; rarely available fresh in
                  markets, but easy to grow
                  and makes an attractive gar-
                  den plant; available dried

Pimentos   Bright red, usually available
                  canned, sweet and mild; also
                  good for adding touches of
                  color

Bell Peppers   Green, changing to red when
mature on plant; very mild
and sweet

A number of our recipes call for canned "tomatoes and green chiles," which are stewed tomatoes with hot green peppers. We have found Ro-Tel brand of tomatoes and green chiles to be dependably consistent in quality and degree of hotness.

SPICES

Spices are all important to good TEX-MEX cooking. All the recipes described in this book incorporate spices that are readily available. Stock your shelves with . . . . .

Cumin (or cumino)
Oregano
Cilantro (Coriander leaves or Chinese parsley)
Chili powder

Chili powder is a blend of ground dried peppers, cumin and oregano. Commercial brands vary widely from mild to hot Mexican Style. Find the one to suit your taste.

. . . . . and plant in a corner of your garden or a corner of your kitchen

Parsley
Chervil (uncurly parsley)
Cilantro
Oregano
Pepper plants

Should you have an excess of hot ripe peppers at summer's end, allow peppers to turn red on the plant. Then pick and string with a large needle on a cord for an interesting kitchen decoration. Use one by one all winter long or wire into a wreath for Christmas!

AVOCADOS

There are two main kinds of avocados. The ones grown in Mexico and the Southwest have a heavy dark skin which becomes almost black as it ripens. These are pear-shaped, pear-sized fruits with a seed the size of a large walnut. Avocados grown in Florida and the Caribbean have a thinner brighter green skin and a flesh with a higher water content. The fruit tends to be considerably larger with a seed the size of a lemon. Generally, one Florida avocado equals two California avocados in volume.

Avocado plants may be easily grown from the avocado seeds. Peel away the brown outer covering of the seed to expose the pale seed. With the pointed end up, stick 3 or 4 toothpicks into the seed to act as supports and place in a glass of water as shown. Keep water level high enough to cover the lower half of seed. The seed will sprout. Often sprouting takes as much as 4 to 6 weeks, so please be patient! When the sprout reaches a height of 3 to 4 inches, roots will also have appeared below the seed. Plant in a pot of good rich soil, just to barely cover the seed. Water every other day, as the soil should be moist. When the sprout reaches 6 inches above the soil, cut back to about 4 inches to promote branching. Continue to cut branches back to encourage further branching. The avocado plants have beautiful large leaves and are decorative house trees. Be sure they have plenty of sunlight.

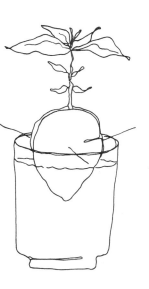

SAUCES AND FILLINGS

Hot Sauce (Salsa)

1 large onion, chopped

1 T. vegetable oil or fresh bacon drippings

2 cups peeled ripe tomatoes, chopped (3 or 4)

3 jalapeño peppers (or more or less to taste) finely chopped

¼ t. salt

1 clove garlic, crushed

Sauté onion in oil until softened. The pieces should not be browned. Add tomatoes, peppers, salt and garlic and simmer for 40 minutes to 1 hour, or until thickened.

When ripe tomatoes are not available, substitute two 10 ounce cans of tomatoes and green chiles and omit the jalapeños.

Salsa Fresca — Uncooked Hot Sauce

6 large ripe tomatoes

1 8 ounce can tomato sauce

2 to 4 jalapeño peppers, seeded and finely chopped

1 bunch green onions, minced (including crisp tops)

1 clove garlic minced (optional)

Salt to taste

2 T. wine vinegar

1 T. olive oil

Peel and finely chop the tomatoes. Add the remaining ingredients and allow to sit several hours before serving.

Save this sauce for summer making when the tomatoes are abundant and full of flavor.

Picante Sauce - ½ cup jalapeños, finely chopped; 1 cup red onions, finely chopped; 1 cup tomatoes, finely chopped; ¼ cup fresh lime juice; 6 T. fresh cilantro, finely chopped; 2 T. olive oil; salt to taste. Combine ingredients and serve at room temperature.

ABOUT TOMATILLOS

*Tomatillos are small, sweet, green Mexican tomatoes. They are not unripe red tomatoes. Tomatillos are available canned and often fresh. When fresh, they are covered with a pale green, papery husk. To prepare fresh tomatillos, remove husk, rinse, and cover with water. Simmer 15 to 20 minutes. May be frozen in cooking liquid.

Tomatillo Salsa

1 large onion, chopped

2 T. oil

2 3½ oz. cans chopped green chiles

4 10 oz. cans tomatillos*

2 garlic cloves, finely minced

1 t. sugar

6 canned or fresh jalapeños, seeded and chopped

Sauté the onion in oil until transparent and limp. Do not brown. Add the remaining ingredients. Simmer about 25 minutes. Yields about 1 quart of sauce.

Green Fanin Sauce (Green Fah-Neen)

1 ripe avocado

1 green onion, chopped

1 cup Tomatillo Salsa (p. 11)

Juice of ½ lime

Water

Salt

Peel and slice the avocado. Place in blender or food processor with onion, tomatillo salsa and lime juice. Puree until smooth. Thin with a little water until the consistency of gravy is reached. Yields approximately 2 cups.

Delicious green dynamite! This sauce is served as a side dish for Mexican Chicken (p. 76), Salpicón (p. 71), Green Enchiladas (p. 64), Soft Tacos (p. 53), and green salad.

Enchilada Sauce

*for cheese, or beef enchiladas
for 24 enchiladas,
approximately 4 cups of sauce*

2 16 oz. cans whole tomatoes

2 T. vegetable oil

1 medium onion, chopped

2 cloves garlic, crushed

3 T. chili powder

½ t. cumin

¼ t. oregano

1 t. salt

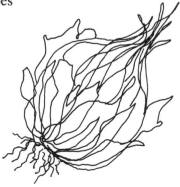

Sauté onion and garlic in oil. Add the remaining ingredients. Cover and simmer 30 minutes. If a smooth, unlumpy sauce is desired, cool and purée in the blender.

Jalapeño Jelly   *Makes 5 6 oz. glasses*

4 or 5 fresh jalapeño peppers, ground

1 green bell pepper, ground

1 cup apple cider vinegar

5 cups sugar

6 oz. liquid fruit pectin

Remove the stems and seeds from the peppers. Place in blender with water for easy blending, drain. Combine peppers, vinegar and sugar in a 3 quart saucepan. Bring to a boil and boil 4 minutes. Remove from heat and skim off foam. Add liquid pectin and stir. Pour into hot sterilized containers, seal with paraffin.

Pickled Fresh Jalapeño Peppers   *2 pints*

20 fresh jalapeño peppers

1 cup apple cider vinegar

¼ cup olive oil

1 t. salt

1 t. pickling spices

Wash jalapeño peppers and pack tightly in pint jars. Combine remaining ingredients in a saucepan and bring to a boil. Pour over peppers leaving about 1 inch air space. Seal jars and process 10 minutes in hot water bath.

HOW TO COOK A CHICKEN FOR FILLINGS

Boil 4 quarts of water. Rinse a 3 pound chicken well in cold water. Place the breast down in the boiling water. Add 2 teaspoons salt, 1 medium onion sliced, 2 ribs celery sliced with leaves, and 1 carrot. Return to a boil. Reduce the heat and simmer 20 minutes. Turn the chicken back side down and simmer 15 minutes more. Cool in the broth at least 30 minutes, then debone. A 3 pound chicken yields 3½ cups of boned chopped chicken.

To cook chicken breasts, follow the same procedure but cook only 20 minutes (no need to turn) and allow to cool in broth and debone. Six breast halves yield about 3 cups.

Cut up the boned chicken with kitchen scissors — the meat will be more tender and less stringy!

Chicken, Tomato & Green Chiles   *12 servings*

4 cups cooked chicken

1 clove garlic, minced

1 medium onion, finely chopped

2 tomatoes, peeled & chopped

1   4 oz. can chopped green chiles

½ t. salt

¼ t. pepper

Sauté onion in 2 tablespoons vegetable oil until soft.   Add tomatoes, garlic and green chiles.   Simmer 10 minutes.   Add chicken and salt & pepper.

Seasoned Chicken

3 cups chicken cooked, boned, cubed

1 cup sour cream (or ½ cup chicken broth—for weight watchers)

1 T. lime juice

1 jalapeño pepper, finely minced (more or less, as desired)

2 to 3 T. green onion, finely minced

1½ t. cumin

Mix together, and marinate a few hours or overnight.

Spiced Ground Beef

1½ lbs. ground beef

1½ T. chili powder

1 t. cumin

½ t. oregano

¼ t. red pepper

½ t. salt

Brown beef in 1 tablespoon oil and add spices. Simmer over low heat 20 to 30 minutes. Add a little water if the mixture gets too dry.

MENUS

SMALL DINNER PARTIES

Tacos

Green Enchiladas

Tamales

Lemon Sherbert atop Baked Bananas

* * * * * * * *

Gazpacho

Fajitas

Pinto Beans

Pralines

* * * * * * * * *

Tortillas Soup

Pico de Gallo

Chicken Portuguese

Tortilla Strips   Rice

Sherbert

DINNER FOR 8 COUPLES (everyone brings a dish)

Picadillo   Nachos

Chicken Chalupas

Beef Enchiladas

Chilaquiles

Pinto Beans

Chilled Fresh Fruits

*   *   *   *   *   *   *   *   *   *

FEAST FOR 12 TO 15 COUPLES (everyone brings a dish)

Chili con Queso   Empanadas   Hot Sauce with Tostados

Gazpacho

Chiles Relleños

Chalupas

Green Enchiladas and Chicken Enchiladas

Salpicón

Tamales

Pralines and Ice Cream

*   *   *   *   *   *   *   *   *   *

SUNDAY NIGHT SUPPER (or Football Game Party)

Chili con Queso with Tostados

Chili

Rice   Pinto Beans

Fresh Tortillas with Butter

Guacamole on a bed of Chopped Lettuce

Sherbert or Fresh Fruit

LUNCHEONS

Gazpacho

Soft Tacos with Chicken

Mango Salad

* * * * * * * * * *

Tacos Dorados

Green Enchiladas

Avocado Salad

* * * * * * * * * *

BRUNCH

Huevos Rancheros

Tamales

Beef Enchiladas

Chilaquiles

Fresh Fruit

* * * * * * * * * *

Eggs Mexicali

Black Beans

Chorizo

Tossed Salad with Oranges and Red Onions

Sherbert

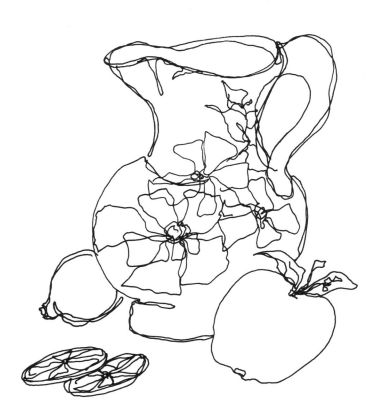

DRINKS

A short but important note about BEER. Plenty of ice cold beer is a must when entertaining with TEX-MEX food!

It is generally a good idea to have two varieties available, one perhaps a light domestic beer, the other a more heavily bodied, imported Mexican brand, such as Carta Blanca.

Tequila Sunrises (for 12)

8 cups of orange juice

12 oz. of tequila

½ cup grenadine syrup

Combine ingredients. Serve over ice and garnish with orange slices.

Red Sangria

½ gallon Burgundy or any dry red wine

2 apples—cored, sliced and unpeeled

2 lemons, sliced thin

2 limes, sliced thin

½ gallon (2 qts.) soda water

½ cup frozen lemonade concentrate or ½ cup sugar

Margaritas (for 8)

8 oz. tequila

6 oz. triple sec liqueur

¾ cup fresh lime juice

coarse or kosher salt

lime slices to garnish

Rub the rim of a cocktail glass with lime and then dip into a saucer of salt. Generously coat the rim. Combine the lime juice, triple sec, and tequila and pour into the glass with ice.

White Sangria

½ gallon dry white wine

2 apples — cored, sliced and unpeeled

½ lemon, sliced thin

1 orange, sliced thin

1 lime, sliced thin

2 fresh peaches, sliced (when available)

½ gallon (2 qts.) soda water

½ cup frozen lemonade concentrate or ½ cup sugar

This is a refreshing summer-time drink and it won't stain carpets or linens like red wine sangria.

APPETIZERS

Stuffed Jalapeño Chiles

Seed whole MILD jalapeños. Make a lengthwise slit to remove seeds or simply cut in half lengthwise and scoop out seeds. Stuff with grated cheese, tuna, salmon or stiff guacamole. Use your leftover bits and pieces! Chill and serve. These may be topped with a little sour cream and sprinkled with paprika.

Cheese and Green Chile Pie   *serves 12 to 15 people*

1 lb. Monterey Jack cheese, grated

1 lb. Longhorn cheese, grated

6 eggs, lightly beaten

1 5 oz. can evaporated milk

2 4 oz. cans chopped green chiles

Combine the cheese, eggs and milk. Line a 9 × 13 pyrex dish with the chiles and cover with the mixture. Bake at 350° for 40 minutes. Cool and cut into bite size squares and serve.

Cut into larger pieces for a first course or use as a luncheon dish — serving 6-8. This may be frozen and reheated.

Nachos

Tostado chips

Grated Longhorn cheese

Place the tostados on a cookie sheet (line with tin foil for easy clean up). Cover each tostado with a spoonful of grated cheese and top with a slice of jalapeño pepper. Broil until the cheese melts, 3 to 5 minutes. Watch closely; nachos burn easily.

Children love these as a snack, without the pepper. Also, a layer of refried beans may be added before the cheese (a little more trouble, but good!).

Fiesta Dip

2 avocados

1 T. mayonnaise

2 T. lemon juice

¼ t. hot sauce

1½ cups Monterey Jack cheese, grated

1½ cups Longhorn cheese, grated

1 4 oz. can chopped black olives

1 medium onion, chopped

½ cup salsa

1 tomato, chopped

½ head lettuce, shredded

Combine mashed avocados, mayonnaise, lemon juice and hot sauce; spread on a large dinner plate (or a shallow bowl similar in size.) Next, layer in order the cheeses, olives, and onions. Then, combine the salsa and chopped tomato and add. Top with the shredded lettuce. This dish can be made in the morning and served in the evening.

Empanadas   *pastry for 60 empanadas*

1 cup softened butter

2 3 oz. packages softened cream cheese

2 cups all-purpose flour

Cream butter and cheese. Blend in the flour. Form into a ball, wrap and chill overnight. Remove from the refrigerator 30 minutes prior to using. Roll out half of the dough ⅛ inch thick on a floured board. Cut out rounds with a large frozen juice can.

Fillings

1. Seasoned ground beef (p. 15)

2. Picadillo (p. 28)

3. Leftover chili

4. Seasoned chicken (p. 15)

Place a rounded teaspoon on the dough. Fold, moisten edge with water and seal with fork prongs. Bake at 400° for 12 to 15 minutes. Make these ahead and freeze. Place newly made, uncooked empanadas on a cookie sheet. Put in the freezer until hardened and the slip into plastic bags. Then add 3 to 5 minutes to cooking time.

Try making larger empanadas for a main course — serve with a green salad and Texican Squash (p. 85).

Quesadillas   *serves 6*

6 8-inch flour tortillas

8 oz. Monterey Jack cheese, grated

1 4 oz. can chopped green chiles

Place the flour tortillas on a cookie sheet. Sprinkle with cheese and top with 1 tablespoon chopped chiles or several slices of jalapeño peppers. Chopped onions and leftover taco filling can be added. Bake at 400° for 10 minutes. Cut into wedges and serve. Quesadillas can also be made on a griddle. Lightly butter the tortilla and place buttered side down on a hot griddle. Top with cheese and chiles. When the cheese melts, remove to a serving platter.

Children love these — but easy on jalapeños for the kiddie batch.

Chili con Queso   *serves 24*

1 lb. Velveeta cheese

1 large onion, chopped

1 T. vegetable oil

1 T. flour

1 T. chili powder

1 clove garlic (optional), minced

1 10 oz. can tomatoes and green chiles

1 chopped jalapeño pepper (optional)

Sauté onion and garlic in oil until transparent. Add flour and chili powder. Cook 1 minute. Add tomatoes and green chiles and cook until sauce is thickened. Add cheese in chunks and cook until melted. Serve hot in a chafing dish with tostados. Yields 4 cups.

Chili con Queso can also serve as a sauce for hamburgers and hot dogs. Add a cupful to cream of corn soup for a super lunch dish. Use as a sauce for leftover chicken. Make ahead, refrigerate to use as needed!

Green Chile Slices *2 dozen*

1 cup cheddar cheese, grated

½ cup flour

4 oz. butter, melted

¼ t. salt

1 4 oz. can chopped green chiles

Mix cheese, flour and salt together. Add butter and knead until blended. Roll dough out thinly into a rectangular shape on a lightly floured board. Drain chiles and spread on dough. Roll dough like a jelly roll. Cover and chill. Slice and bake on a lightly greased cookie sheet. Bake at 350° for 10 to 12 minutes.

Jalapeño Bean Dip *serves 12*

2 cups refried beans

½ lb. Monterey Jack cheese

1 medium onion, chopped and sautéed in 1 T. oil

3-4 medium jalapeños finely chopped

Combine all ingredients in a double boiler and stir until heated thoroughly. Serve in a chafing dish with tostados. Yields 1 quart of dip.

Picadillo   *serves 25 for dip*

1½ lbs. lean ground beef

1 medium onion, chopped

2 T. vegetable oil

1 t. salt

1 clove garlic, crushed

1-2 t. chili powder

1 8 oz. can tomato sauce

1 8 oz. can mushrooms, drained

1 16 oz. can tomatoes

2 T. vinegar

1 t. sugar

½ t. ground cumin

1 t. ground cinnamon

½ cup raisins

Pinch of ground cloves

½ cup sliced almonds

Cook the onions in oil until soft. Then, add ground beef and cook until browned. Add the rest of the ingredients except the almonds. Stir well and simmer covered for 1½ hours. Stir in almonds just before serving. Serve in a chafing dish (to keep warm) with tostados or Doritos. This is best if made the day before serving. Yields about 2 quarts.

Picadillo stands alone as an appetizer or main dish served with rice. It is perfect as a filling for empanadas or for Chiles Relleños (p. 68).

Guacamole   *serves 6*

2 ripe avocados, mashed

½ peeled tomato, finely chopped

2 T. grated onion

2 T. fresh cilantro, finely chopped (optional)

2 T. lemon juice

Salt and pepper to taste

2 dashes of Tabasco sauce

Combine all the ingredients and mix well. Return the avocado seeds to the mixture and cover tightly to prevent discoloration. Yields 1½ to 2 cups.

Serve Guacamole as a dip with chips, on a bed of lettuce garnished with tomatoes for a salad or on Chalupas.

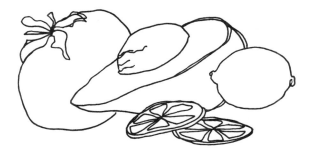

Leftover Taco Fixings - Line cookie sheet, pie plate or pizza pan with tostados. Sprinkle with meat mixture, chopped onions, chopped tomatoes, shredded Longhorn cheese and whatever else you like. Top with slices of Monterey Jack cheese. Bake at 400° until cheese bubbles, about 15 or 20 minutes.

Guacamole   *serves 30*

12 ripe avocados, peeled

1 to 2 t. ground coriander

Salt and pepper to taste

Hot pepper sauce to taste

Juice of 4 limes

2 ripe tomatoes, peeled and chopped

1 jalapeño, seeded and chopped

1 small onion, grated

Mash avocados and add the remaining ingredients. Place several avocado seeds in the guacamole to prevent browning and cover tightly. Yields 5½ to 6 cups.

Meat Balls in Chili con Queso   *serves 36*

1½ lbs. lean ground beef

1 package taco seasoning mix

1 medium onion, finely chopped

1½ cups crushed tostados

¼ cup Hot Sauce (p. 10)

Chili con Queso (p. 26)

Mix the ground beef with taco seasoning mix, onions, crushed tostados and hot sauce. Form into cherry sized balls and brown. Add the cooked meat balls to hot Chili con Queso. Serve in a chafing dish.

Make ahead and freeze meat balls and Chili con Queso separately.

Mexican Pie

2 cups refried pinto beans (pp. 87 & 89)

3 avocados, mashed

2 T. lemon juice

5 T. diced onions

⅛ t. cayenne pepper

½ t. salt

1 cup sour cream

½ cup mayonnaise

½ t. garlic powder

1 t. ground cumin

½ t. hot pepper sauce

½ t. chili powder

2 cups Longhorn cheese, grated

6 scallions, chopped

3 medium tomatoes, seeded & chopped

1 4 oz. can chopped black olives

Spread refried beans on the bottom of a 9 x 13 casserole.
Combine the avocados, lemon juice, 2 tablespoons diced onions,
cayenne pepper and salt. Spread on the beans. Mix sour cream,
mayonnaise, cumin, garlic powder, hot pepper sauce, chili powder
and 3 tablespoons diced onions. Spread on the avocado mixture.
Cover the sour cream mixture with cheese, scallions, tomatoes and
black olives. This can be made a day ahead.

Ceviche   *serves 6*

1 lb. fresh bay or sea scallops or boneless white fish fillets, cut in small squares

½ cup fresh lime juice

2 jalapeño peppers, seeded & chopped

2 medium tomatoes, peeled & chopped

1 avocado, chopped

6 scallions, chopped

4 T. fresh cilantro, chopped

¼ cup olive oil

1 T. white wine vinegar

salt & pepper

The day before serving ,wash scallops or fish, place in bowl and cover with lime juice. Tightly cover container and refrigerate overnight. Next day, remove scallops with slotted spoon and set aside. Stir the avocado in the lime juice, remove and add to the scallops. Reserve 1 or 2 tablespoons lime juice. Add the remaining ingredients to the scallops and avocados. Season with salt and pepper and lime juice, if needed. Cover and chill til serving time.

SOUPS

Black Bean Soup

1 lb. dried black beans

1 ham bone (or ¼ lb. salt pork chopped into match sticks)

2 medium onions, chopped

1 carrot, chopped

1 stalk celery, chopped

1 or 2 cloves garlic, crushed

1½ t. salt

1 t. pepper

1 bay leaf or laurel leaf

¼ cup wine vinegar, optional

Wash the beans and pick out the rocks. Place the beans with all the ingredients (except vinegar) in 3 quarts water in heavy pot. Bring to a boil and simmer 1½ to 2 hours until the beans "lose their shape." Pureé. Add vinegar, if desired. Add more water or stock if too thick. Remove bones and bay leaf. Serve!

Top with a spoonful of sour cream and a dusting of chili powder. Or, serve garnished with sieved hard boiled egg, finely chopped green onions or a lemon slice.

Pumpkin Soup (Squash Soup)   *serves 10*

1 large onion, chopped

4 cups cooked pumpkin or winter squash

3 cups chicken broth

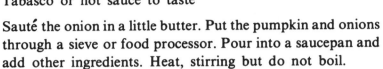

2 cups milk or light cream

Salt and pepper to taste

Tabasco or hot sauce to taste

Sauté the onion in a little butter. Put the pumpkin and onions through a sieve or food processor. Pour into a saucepan and add other ingredients. Heat, stirring but do not boil.

Serve hot with a spoon of whipped cream or cold with a spoon of yogurt. Garnish with minced, tender spring onion and a sprinkle of chili powder. Do not prepare more than 24 hours ahead.

Year-'Round Gazpacho   *serves 5 to 6*

2 1 lb. cans stewed tomatoes

2 t. seasoned salt

2 to 3 mild jalapeño peppers, seeded and chopped

Combine all the ingredients and blend in the blender or food processor until smooth. Serve well chilled with a choice of chopped cucumbers, green pepper, onions and tomatoes, crumbled bacon and croutons

Wonderful for quantity making!

Summer Gazpacho   *serves 12 to 16*

8 large tomatoes, peeled

1 large green pepper

2 large cucumbers, peeled

1 red onion

5 spring onions

4 large cloves garlic, pressed

2 T. Accent

2 cups V-8 juice or tomato juice

1 qt. water

⅓ cup vinegar

½ cup olive oil

1½ T. salt

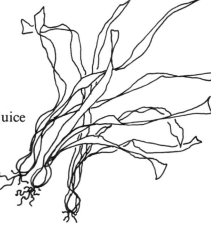

Freshly ground pepper to taste

Chop all the vegetables and combine with the rest of the ingredients. This will keep for several days in the refrigerator. Serves 12 to 16.

Save this recipe for those fresh, tasty summer vegetables.

Green Gazpacho   *serves 6 to 8*

3 cucumbers

2 cups green tomatillas or one 16 oz. can

1 green Bell pepper

1 small onion chopped (or 4 spring onions with tops)

2 sprigs parsley

1 cup chicken broth

1 T. vinegar

Salt and pepper to taste

Hot sauce, if you wish

Blend or process all the ingredients. Chill well. Stir and serve with croutons.

Homemade Croutons

½ cup olive oil

2 cloves garlic, peeled

3 slices bread

Soak the garlic in the oil several hours, if possible. Cut the crust off the bread. Slice the bread into squares about the size of a dime. Heat the oil over medium heat; add bread cubes. Sauté until golden brown, turning frequently. Drain well. Sprinkle lightly with salt. Makes 1½ cups.

Once you have tried these, you'll never use the store-bought kind again!

Tortilla Soup   *serves 4 to 6*

4 cups homemade chicken broth

4 oz. tomato sauce

1 medium onion, chopped

Salt and pepper to taste

4 tortillas

¼ cup vegetable oil

Chopped fresh cilantro to garnish (or parsley)

Cut the tortillas into strips and fry in oil until crisp. In the same pan cook the onions until limp. Add the chicken broth and tomato sauce and bring to a boil. Simmer 30 minutes. Place half the tortillas in the soup. Use the remainder instead of crackers.

Avocaté Soup   *serves 8*

4 ripe avocados

2½ cups of chicken broth

Juice of 2 lemons

Salt to taste

1 T. chopped onion

1 cup milk

2 dashes Tabasco or more to taste

1 or 2 T. rum (optional)

Toasted sesame seeds to garnish

Pureé avocados, a little at a time, with some broth in a blender or food processor. Pour into a bowl and add the remaining ingredients. Seal tightly and chill 2 to 3 hours before serving.

SALADS

Taco Salad *serves 8 to 12*

1 lb. lean ground beef

1 T. chili powder

½ t. ground cumin

1 clove garlic, pressed

½ t. oregano

¼ t. dry red pepper

2 tomatoes, chopped

½ cup onion, chopped

1 cup grated sharp cheese

1½ heads iceburg lettuce

1½ cups crushed Fritos

2 avocados, peeled and sliced

Sauté the beef with the seasonings until done. Drain very well. Keep at room temperature. Combine and toss all the ingredients with the dressing. Dressing: Mix 2 tablespoons lemon juice and ½ cup of mayonnaise.

A great and relatively thinning luncheon — a nice change from chef salad.

39

Taco Salad con Queso   *serves 8 to 12*

1½ lbs. lean ground beef

1 T. chili powder

1 t. salt

1 t. cumin

1½ cups diced onion

1 cup celery, minced

1 cup green pepper, minced

3 cloves garlic, pressed

1 lb. Velveeta cheese

½ to 1 10 oz. can tomatoes and green chiles

1 large head iceberg lettuce, chopped

2 large tomatoes, chopped

1 6 oz. package Doritos or tostados

Brown the meat with the chili powder, salt and cumin. Sauté the onions, celery, green pepper, and garlic until limp. In a saucepan, melt cheese, add tomatoes and green chiles and keep warm. Place the chopped lettuce and tomatoes in a large bowl. Add the meat and vegetables and toss. Then add the broken Doritos and pour the hot cheese mixture over all.

Mango Salad

3 3 oz. packages lemon Jello

1 29 oz. can mangos, drained (save liquid)

3 cups boiling liquid (mango liquid plus water to make 3 cups)

1 8 oz. package cream cheese

Juice of 2 limes

Rind of 1 lime, grated

Dissolve Jello in boiling liquid. Combine mangos and cream cheese in blender and blend until creamy. Add to Jello and stir in lime juice. Pour into a greased mold and chill overnight. Unmold and serve on bed of shredded lettuce.

Molded Avocado Salad

5 avocados (2 if using large Florida variety)

2½ to 3 cups fresh grapefruit sections (2 large grapefruit)

½ cup fresh lemon juice

¼ t. salt

1 T. sugar

1 cup fresh grapefruit juice

2 envelopes unflavored gelatin (2 T.)

¼ cup cold water

½ cup boiling water

Peel and pureé 4 avocados, save one avocado to slice for garnish. Soften gelatin in cold water, add boiling water and stir until dissolved. Add the other ingredients which have been chilled. Pour into a 6 cup mold which has been rinsed with cool water. Chill until firm. Unmold and garnish with avocado slices.

Pico de Gallo (Rooster's Beak)   *serves 8*

4 ripe avocados

2 tomatoes

1 medium onion

1 clove garlic, crushed

3 T. lemon juice

1½ T. juice from canned jalapeños

2 T. olive oil

2 T. fresh cilantro or 1 t. dried

Salt and pepper to taste

Chop the avocados, tomatoes and onions. Add the remaining ingredients and mix well. Make this several hours prior to serving. Refrigerate covered.

Try spooning Pico de Gallo onto hot, buttered tortillas. Roll and eat! Lovely vegetarian luncheon dish.

Molded Gazpacho Salad

4 large peeled, ripe tomatoes

1 small cucumber

1 small onion

¼ cup green pepper

1 to 2 T. vinegar

2 cups V-8 juice (or tomato juice)

Hot sauce or Tabasco to taste

Salt to taste

¾ cup chicken broth

2 envelopes unflabored gelatin (2 T.)

Chop fine, blend or process the tomatoes, cucumber, green pepper and onion. Moisten the gelatin in ¼ cup broth. Then add ½ cup boiling broth. Next add the V-8 juice and the remaining ingredients. Pour into individual molds or one large ring mold. Refrigerate overnight or until firm. Serve on a bed of shredded lettuce. Garnish, as desired, with chopped cucumber, peppers, hard cooked eggs, parsley, scallions and avocado.

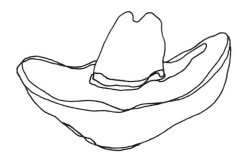

EGG DISHES

Huevos con Papas, MMM Eggs *eggs for two*

2 small potatoes (size of lemons), chopped

1 T. bacon drippings or oil

2 T. chopped onion

1 T. chopped Bell pepper

1 tomato, chopped

4 eggs, beaten

½ t. ground coriander

½ t. salt

Hot sauce (p. 10)

In a skillet sauté potatoes in bacon drippings or oil until tender. Add chopped onion, pepper and tomato and sauté until tender. Stir in beaten eggs with salt and coriander. Cook and stir until eggs are set. Serve immediately with hot sauce and fresh flour tortillas (p. 91)

Easy one dish meal. Garnish with fresh parsley for an attractive luncheon dish.

Huevos Rancheros Migas   *serves 2*

4 eggs, beaten

2 T. bacon drippings

½ t. Tabasco sauce, or more to taste

2 T. onion, finely chopped

2 T. green pepper, finely chopped

¼ cup sharp cheese, grated

6 to 8 tostados, crumbled

Heat the bacon drippings. Add the eggs, Tabasco sauce, onions, and peppers. Cook over medium heat. When the eggs are almost done, reduce the heat and add the cheese and then the tostados.

Migas means crumbs.

Huevos Rancheros   *serves 6 to 8*

1 dozen eggs

1 t. salt

2 cups Hot Sauce (p. 10)

Pour the hot sauce into a rectangular 2 quart pyrex dish and heat in the oven 10 minutes at 325°. Break the eggs into a bowl and add salt and stir. Pour into the pyrex dish on top of the sauce. Sprinkle with chopped fresh parsley. Bake at 325° for about 20 minutes or until eggs are set. Serve immediately with crisp hot tostados.

Great for hangovers served with Bloody Marys and an extra bowl of hot sauce!

Skillet Huevos Rancheros   *serves 2*

¼ cup chopped onion (½ small onion)

1 T. bacon drippings

1 tomato, peeled, if time permits, and chopped

4 eggs, beaten

Salt and pepper

Hot Sauce (p. 10)

Sauté onion in bacon drippings until transparent. Add chopped tomato, cook for 2 minutes. Add beaten eggs and salt and pepper to skillet, stirring until set. Spoon on hot sauce, as much as you dare! Serve immediately with tostados and Chorizo (p. 74).

A great cold weather breakfast—one to get you rolling in any weather!

Eggs Mexicali   *serves 6*

3 large tomatoes, peeled, seeded and chopped

1 medium onion, chopped

2 garlic, pressed

3 T. olive oil

4 T. chopped green chiles

1½ t. oregano

1½ t. coriander

1 t. salt

3 avocados

2 T. grated onion

3 T. lime or lemon juice

2 T. olive oil

12 tortillas

6 poached eggs

1 cup grated Monterey Jack cheese

Sauce: Sauté the onions and garlic in the oil until limp. Add the tomatoes, chiles, oregano, coriander and salt. Simmer for 30 minutes. Mash the avocado and add the onion, lime or lemon juice and olive oil. Soften the tortillas in hot oil and drain on paper towel. Using approximately half of the avocado mixture, spread 6 of the tortillas with avocado. Place a tablespoon of the tomato sauce on each avocado spread tortilla. Place in a 9" by 13" casserole dish. Top with the remaining 6 tortillas and spread with the remaining avocado mixture. Place an egg on each top layer tortilla and top with the remaining tomato sauce and the grated Monterey Jack cheese. Bake at 450° for 4 to 5 minutes, until the cheese is melted.

This is a lovely dish for an elegant brunch, but for a hearty supper, use 2 poached eggs on each top layer tortilla.

Huevo Ranchero   *serves 1*

1 fried egg

1 crisp fried tortilla

Hot sauce to taste

Grated sharp cheese

Place a fried egg on top of the tortilla. Spoon on hot sauce and top with grated cheese. Place under the broiler until the cheese is melted.

MAIN DISHES

Tacos

The best known Mexican dish — The Mexican Sandwich. Begin with a crisp fried taco shell (p. 6) (warmed in a 250° oven for 5 minutes). Then fill with:

Spiced Ground Beef (p. 15) or shredded chicken

Grated Longhorn cheese

Chopped fresh tomatoes

Shredded iceberg lettuce

Chopped onion

Hot Sauce

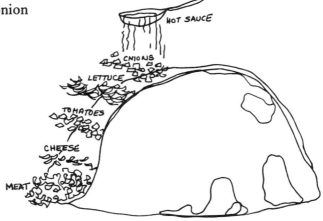

Vegetarians make tacos substituting refried beans for meat!

Chalupas Compuestas

Chalupas can be used as a salad, as a "first course," as a whole meal for lunch, a light Sunday supper, or a "build your own" for buffet.

Begin with a crisp fried chalupa shell (warmed in a 250° oven for 5 minutes). Assemble with a layer of each of the following:

Beef Chalupas

Hot Refried Pinto Beans (p. 87)

Seasoned Ground Beef (p. 15)

Grated Longhorn cheese

*Hot sauce (p. 10)

Chopped fresh tomatoes

Chopped onion

Shredded iceburg lettuce

Guacamole

*Hot sauce

GUACAMOLE
LETTUCE
TOMATO
ONION
HOT SAUCE
CHEESE
SHREDDED CHICKEN
SOUR CREAM
BEANS
TORTILLA

Chicken Chalupas

Hot Refried Black Beans (p. 88)

Sour cream

Shredded chicken

Grated Monterey Jack cheese

*Hot sauce

Chopped onion

Chopped fresh tomato

Shredded lettuce

Guacamole

*Hot sauce

*There are differing opinions as to when the hot sauce should be applied — let your taste be your guide — some folks apply hot sauce at both points to keep *all* the experts happy!

Soft Tacos

Heat a griddle to medium high temperature. Brush one side of the tortilla lightly with vegetable oil and place the oiled side down on the griddle and brush the other side with oil. Allow about 30 seconds cooking time per side. Remove tortillas as they cook and stack them between 2 folded dish towels to keep them warm or place them in a tortilla warmer. Place 2 tablespoons filling in each tortilla and fold. For soft chicken tacos use either Chicken , Tomatoes & Green Chiles (p. 14) or Seasoned Chicken (p. 15). For soft beef tacos use Spiced Ground Beef (p. 15) or leftover chili. Serve with any or all of the following: grated cheese, chopped tomatoes, chopped onion, shredded lettuce, salsa.

Tamales   *2½ dozen*

First prepare corn husks by soaking in warm water 3 to 4
hours or overnight.

Filling

3 full cups cooked, lean pork roast
  (save some of the fat trimmings)

1 10 oz. can tomatoes and green chiles

1 medium onion, chopped

1 or 2 cloves garlic, pressed

1 T. chili powder

1 t. salt

Combine the tomatoes and green chiles, onion, garlic, chili
powder and salt in a saucepan and simmer 30 minutes until
thickened. Shred the pork (a food processor is ideal for this).
Mix the sauce and meat together and set aside. Chicken, turkey or beef may be used instead of pork.

Dough

3 cups Masa

1½ cups shortening
  (use the fat trimmings from the pork for added flavor)

½ cup chicken broth

Place the Masa, shortening and pork trimmings in the food
processor and gradually add the chicken broth. Process until
mixture is very fluffy (masa will float on top when dropped
into a cup of cold water). More broth can be added, a tablespoon at a time if masa seems too thick to spread easily.

To Assemble

Spread husks with masa, placing 1 heaping tablespoon masa in middle of husk and spreading as shown. Spread 1 heaping tablespoon filling, as shown. Roll beginning with filled edge and fold up bottom of husk. Place on flat surface with fold underneath.

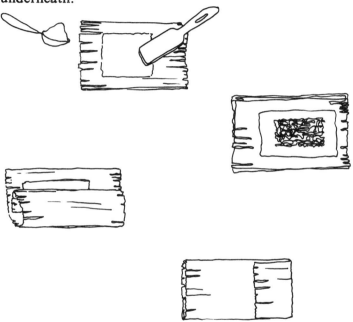

Steaming

Steam cook tamales by placing them upright on folded end in steamer. To improvise a steamer, invert a pie tin, punched with holes as a support for another foil pie tin (punch numerous small holes to let the steam circulate) and place in a large kettle. Pour about 1 inch of water in the kettle; cover tightly and steam 2 hours. Check water level frequently. Tamales are done when one can be unrolled, clear and free of the husk.

Don't eat the corn husk!

Venison Tamales

Venison is usually very lean, but is delicious as a tamale filling when mixed with an equal amount of pork. Use 1½ cups of cooked venison (leftover from a roast) and 1½ cups of pork to make 3 cups of meat for the tamale filling and proceed with the tamale recipe.

Duck Tamales

Hunters in your family? Or have you leftover Long Island duckling? Use 3 cups cooked and shredded duck in place of the pork for the filling.

Be careful to remove all bones!

Three recipes for Beef Enchiladas!!! All terrific!

We find that 16 enchiladas fit perfectly into a 9" × 13" pyrex casserole dish.

Beef Enchiladas I   serves 8

Sauce

8 T. flour

½ cup vegetable oil

2 or 3 T. chili powder

4 t. cumin

2 t. salt

2 cloves garlic, crushed

5½ cups hot water

Brown the flour in a pan in a 500° oven (about 20 minutes — it will look like cocoa). Place the browned flour in a pan with the oil and add all the other ingredients except the water.

Blend over low heat until smooth. Add the water slowly, stirring constantly. Simmer 2 to 3 hours, or until fairly thick. Cool and refrigerate overnight. Do not try to double this recipe.

Meat

1 lb. lean ground beef

½ t. cumin

1 clove garlic, crushed

½ t. salt

2 T. hot taco sauce

1 T. water, if needed

Brown the meat. Add the other ingredients and simmer for 20 to 30 minutes. Add water, if necessary, to keep moist.

2 onions, chopped

1 lb. grated sharp cheese

16 tortillas

Prepare the tortillas for enchiladas (p. 5). Place the meat mixture, onions, and cheese on the tortilla, roll and place in a casserole. Heat the sauce and pour over the enchiladas. Top with cheese. Bake at 350° for 20 to 30 minutes.

Careful — don't overcook these!

Beef Enchiladas II   *serves 12*

3 lb. boneless chuck roast

Enchilada Sauce   (1½ recipes p. 12)

½ lb. grated Monterey Jack cheese

24 tortillas

Liberally sprinkle the chuck roast with garlic salt, pepper and
cumin. Bake in a covered pan at 275° for about 4 hours or
until meat easily falls apart. When cool enough to handle,
shred beef and place in a bowl with one half of the enchilada
sauce. Marinate overnight. Soften the tortillas in oil for
enchiladas (p. 5). Place 1½ to 2 tablespoons of meat mixture
in each tortilla and roll. Place in a rectangular casserole, pour
the sauce over and top with grated cheese. Bake at 350° for
20 to 30 minutes.
*For an attractive touch top with pepitas, toasted pumpkin
seeds.*

Beef Enchiladas III   *serves 12*

2 dozen tortillas

1½ lbs. extra sharp cheddar cheese, or Longhorn, grated

2 cups cooking oil

Sauce

1 10 oz. can tomatoes and green chiles

1 16 oz. can tomatoes

1 clove garlic, crushed

2 T. chili powder

1 T. cumin seed

4 cups beef boullion

Salt and pepper

Beef Filling

2 lbs. lean ground beef

1 onion, chopped

2 T. chili powder

1 T. cumin seed

Salt and pepper

Sauce – Put tomatoes, garlic, chili powder and cumin seed in the blender. Blend for 10 seconds in two batches, if necessary. Pour into saucepan and add beef boullion and simmer for 20 minutes. Correct seasoning.

Beef Filling — Sauté onions in a little oil until golden. Add the meat and brown. Drain off the fat and add salt, pepper, chili powder, cumin and 1 cup of sauce. Soften the tortillas in oil and then dip in the sauce. Fill with about 2 tablespoons meat and 2 tablespoons cheese and roll. Place one layer side by side in 2 shallow rectangular casseroles. Sprinkle generously with grated cheese. (This much may be completed ahead or even frozen if desired. Freeze the sauce separately.)

Pour the remaining sauce over each casserole just before cooking. Cover very loosely with foil and heat at 325° for 20 to 30 minutes. Do not overcook.

Our favorite *recipes for Chicken Enchiladas!*

Chicken Enchiladas   *serves 18*
                          use 2 9″ × 13″ pyrex casseroles

2 chickens (4 to 5 lbs. each)

2 ribs celery, cut in pieces

2 carrots, cut in pieces

2 garlic cloves, peeled

Salt and pepper

1 to 2 T. ground cumin

2 green peppers, chopped

2 medium onions, chopped

3 T. vegetable oil

1 4 oz. can green chiles, chopped

2 t. chili powder

1 t. garlic powder

1 lb. sharp cheddar cheese, grated

32 tortillas

2 cups chicken broth

1 5 oz. can evaporated milk

1 can condensed cream of chicken soup

1 10 oz. can tomatoes and green chiles

½ lb. Monterey Jack cheese, grated

Make a broth with the celery, carrots, garlic salt and pepper
and water to just cover. Add the chickens and poach them
until tender, about 1½ hours. Remove chickens from broth.

When cool, remove meat from bones and shred it. Stir cumin into broth and put it aside.

Sauté the green peppers and onions in oil. Scrape into a bowl and mix in green chiles. Combine chili and garlic powders and put into an empty spice bottle or another container with a shaker top.

Use two 9″ × 13″ pyrex casserole dishes. Pour ½ cup broth in bottom of each casserole. Dip a tortilla in hot chicken broth briefly to soften it. Then spread on it small amounts of chicken, peppers and onion mixture, grated cheese, and a generous shake of the chili and garlic powder seasoning. Roll up the tortillas placing each enchilada in the casserole as it is rolled, making a single layer.

Pour 2 cups of broth with the evaporated milk and condensed soup into a saucepan. Stir together and heat to make a sauce. Pour it over the enchiladas. Add the tomatoes (undrained) and place the casserole in a preheated 325° oven. Cook for 45 minutes. Add Monterey Jack for final 10 minutes.

The tortillas in this recipe can be softened in hot oil instead of hot chicken broth.

Chicken Enchiladas   *serves 8*

3 cups cooked, diced chicken (p. 14)

1 10 oz. can tomatoes and green chiles

1 16 oz. can of tomatoes

1 clove garlic, crushed

1 large onion, chopped

¾ t. coriander

1 t. salt

2 cups sour cream

1 lb. sharp cheese, grated

16 tortillas

Sauce — Combine tomatoes, garlic, onion, coriander and salt in a blender. Pour into a sauce pan and simmer 30 minutes. Remove from heat, cool slightly and stir in sour cream. Soften tortillas in hot oil and then dip in sauce. Spoon chicken and cheese in each tortilla, roll and put in a casserole dish side by side. Just before cooking, pour remaining sauce over enchiladas and sprinkle with cheese. Bake at 325° for 30 minutes.

Green Chicken Enchiladas   *serves 8*

8 chicken breasts (halves) (p. 14)

1 onion

1 clove garlic, peeled

4 10 oz. cans tomatillas

4 green onions

2 jalapeño peppers

1 bunch parsley

2 cloves garlic

2 cups chicken broth
(from cooking of chicken breasts)

½ t. cumin

½ t. pepper

2 T. vegetable oil

¾ lb. Monterey Jack cheese, grated

1 small onion, chopped

16 tortillas

Stew the chicken breasts in water to cover, with onion, garlic, salt and pepper. Cool and shred. Reserve broth. Place shredded chicken, grated cheese and chopped onion in bowl. Toss with fork to combine.

Sauce — In a blender place tomatillas, green onions, jalapeños, parsley, garlic, 2 cups of chicken broth, cumin and pepper. Blend until smooth. Place the oil in a skillet and add the sauce and ½ teaspoon salt. Reduce by one fourth.

Soften tortillas in oil for enchiladas (p. 5). Fill each tortilla with 2 heaping tablespoons onion, shredded cheese and chicken mixture. Arrange in a single layer side by side in a 9″ × 13″ casserole. Pour over the sauce. Bake at 325° for 20 to 30 minutes.

Green Enchiladas (Spinach)   *serves 12*

24 tortillas

4 medium onions, chopped

1½ lbs. Monterey Jack cheese, grated

2 cans cream of chicken soup

1 10 oz. package frozen, chopped spinach, thawed and drained

¼ cup minced green onions

2 or 3 jalapeño peppers, seeded and chopped

¼ t. salt

2 cups sour cream

Combine spinach, green onions, soup and jalapeños in blender and blend until smooth. Add the sour cream. Prepare the tortillas for enchiladas by softening in hot oil (see p. 5). Fill the tortillas with approximately 1 tablespoon onion and 1 heaping tablespoon or more of cheese, and roll. Place in a 9" by 13" casserole and cover with the green spinach sauce. Sprinkle with the remaining cheese. Bake at 325° for 30 minutes.

Enchiladas Suizas   *serves 8*

1 medium onion, chopped

2 T. vegetable oil

1 clove garlic, minced

2 cups tomato sauce

2 4 oz. cans chopped green chiles

3 cups chicken, cooked & chopped

16 tortillas

6 chicken bouillon cubes

3 cups half & half cream

½ lb. Monterey Jack cheese, grated

Sauté onion in oil until soft. Add garlic, tomato sauce, green chiles and chicken. Simmer for 10 minutes and add salt if needed. Soften the tortillas in oil for enchiladas (p. 5). Dissolve bouillon cubes in hot cream. Dip softened tortillas in the cream mixture. Fill with the seasoned chicken. Roll and place seam side down in a 9 x 13 casserole. Pour the remaining cream over the enchiladas and cover with cheese. Bake at 350° for 30 minutes.

Cheese Enchiladas   *serves 8*

24 tortillas

2 medium onions, chopped

1½ lbs. cheese, grated (Longhorn or Monterey Jack, or a combination)

1 recipe Enchilada Sauce   (p. 12)

Soften tortillas in hot oil for enchiladas (see p. 5). Fill each tortilla with a generous heaping tablespoon of cheese and a half of tablespoon onion. Roll. Place in a 9″ by 13″ casserole. Pour the sauce over just before baking and top with the remaining cheese. Bake at 350° for 20 to 30 minutes.

Cheese Enchiladas topped with "leftover" chili and grated cheese are delicious!

Fajitas   *serves 6*

Fajitas (fa HEE tahs) are basically thin slices of marinated, grilled skirt steak topped with a sauce or several condiments and wrapped in a warm flour tortilla. Skirt steak, however, is not readily available in all areas of the country; flank steak is a good substitute. Some suggestions for condiments to serve with Fajitas are salsa or picante sauce, grilled or sautéed onions, Pico de Gallo (p. 42), chopped tomatoes, chopped lettuce, sour cream, shredded cheese, guacamole or sliced avocado. Use your imagination! Fajitas, once filled are rolled and eaten with your hands.

1½ lbs. skirt steak (or flank steak)

½ cup fresh lime juice

3 to 4 cloves garlic, minced

¼ cup olive oil

1 t. salt

½ t. pepper

6 8-inch flour tortillas

If using skirt steak, make sure that the membrane surrrounding the steak has been cut away. Cut the steak in 3 to 4 inch pieces or if using flank steak, leave in one piece. Marinate 4 to 6 hours at room temperature. Grill steak over a hot charcoal and mesquite fire 4 to 5 minutes per side or until desired degree of doneness. Slice steak thinly across the grain. Tightly wrap flour tortillas in foil. Heat at 350° for 15 minutes. Place sliced steak in warm tortillas. Add condiments and roll up.

Another very good marinade for Fajitas is ½ cup papaya juice (available at health food stores) and ½ cup vodka. Marinate the

steak overnight. Pour off the marinade and make a new one of 3
cloves garlic, minced, 1 ½ cups beer, ¼ cup olive oil and salt and
pepper. Marinate 4 or 5 hours at room temperature and grill.

Chicken Fajitas   *serves 6*

1½ to 2 lbs. boneless chicken breasts

¼ cup fresh lime juice

¼ cup tequila

¼ cup olive oil

2 cloves garlic, minced

1 t. salt

½ t. pepper

Combine the lime juice, tequila, olive oil, garlic, salt and pepper.
Marinate chicken breasts 4 to 6 hours in the refrigerator. Grill over
a charcoal and mesquite fire for 8 to 10 minutes per side. Slice in
½ inch strips. Serve in warm flour tortillas with condiments.

A note about mesquite - mesquite is a very hard, fragrant wood that
imparts a delicious flavor to grilled meats. It's generally available
commercially in three forms - chips, chunks and charcoal. Chips
or chunks are simply added to a reqular charcoal fire shortly before
grilling. However, when using mesquite charcoal only, you
should keep in mind that it burns hotter than normal charcoal
briquets.

Chiles Relleños   *serves 12*

(Choice of Picante or Spicy Raisin and Olive Filling)

Picante Filling

1½ lbs. ground beef

1½ T. chili powder

1 t. cumin

½ t. oregano

¼ t. red pepper

1 8 oz. can tomato sauce

1 medium onion, chopped

2 cloves garlic, minced

½ lb. Monterey Jack cheese, grated

Salt and pepper to taste

1 or 2 jalapeño peppers, seeded and chopped

Sauté the onion and garlic in 2 tablespoons oil. Add the beef and brown. Combine the remaining ingredients except cheese. Simmer 30 minutes, then add the cheese stirring until melted.

Spicy Raisin and Olive Filling

1½ lbs. ground beef

1 medium onion, chopped

2 cloves garlic, minced

1 T. parsley

1 cup pecans or walnuts, broken

½ cup raisins

1 dozen olives, chopped

Sauté the onion and garlic in 2 tablespoons oil. Add the beef and brown. Combine the remaining ingredients. Simmer 30 minutes.

3 cans whole green chiles or 12 chiles poblanos (fresh)

If you are using canned chiles, rinse, remove any seeds, and pat dry. For fresh chiles poblanos, roast for 15 minutes at 500° turning until blistered and blackened. The chiles can also be roasted over a gas flame using a long fork. Either way, place the chiles in a paper or plastic bag for 10 minutes to sweat and then peel. Carefully place about 2 tablespoons of filling in the chiles and gently reform.

Batter

1½ cups beer

1½ cups flour

Add beer to flour and wisk until smooth. Allow batter to rest covered and unrefrigerated for at least 3 hours. Roll stuffed chiles in flour, dip in beer batter and fry immediately in vegetable oil heated to 350°. Use about 1 inch oil in a skillet or deep fat fry. Fry until golden brown on both sides and drain on a wire rack over a large brown bag with a cookie sheet under everything. These are best served right away or if you must, place the chiles, wire rack and cookie sheet in a 200° oven for a short time.

Shrimp en Escabeche   *serves 6 to 8*

Sauce

2 T. vinegar

2 T. chili powder

1 cup water

4 cloves garlic, finely minced

2 large onions, chopped

1 t. oregano

1 8 oz. can tomato sauce

2 bay leaves

1 16 oz. can tomatoes or 2 cups ripe, peeled, chopped tomatoes

Boil vinegar, chili powder and water together for 10 minutes. Add remaining ingredients and simmer 15 to 20 minutes.

Shrimp:

4 qts. water

1 T. salt

1 lemon, sliced thinly

3 large ribs of celery with leaves

3 lbs. raw, unpeeled shrimp

Peel and devein shrimp. Bring water, with salt, lemon and celery to a rolling boil. Add the peeled shrimp. Allow water to return to boil, and cook for 3 to 4 minutes. Taste for doneness after three minutes. Smaller shrimp cook faster than large shrimp . . . vary cooking time to match size, continue tasting until done. Do not overcook! Add shrimp to sauce, salt to taste. Serve over hot steamy rice.

Salpicón   *serves 16 to 20*

8 lbs. top sirloin roast

2 cloves garlic

2 bay leaves

1 T. black peppercorns

5 or 6 dried red chiles or 2 T. crushed, dried red chiles, available at spice counter of supermarket

1 16 oz. can tomatoes

½ cup chopped fresh cilantro

Salt and pepper to taste

8 oz. Italian salad dressing*

1½ cups chopped green chiles

½ lb. Monterey Jack cheese, cut into ½ inch squares

2 avocados, peeled and sliced

¼ cup fresh parsley

Place beef in a large pot. Cover with water and add garlic, bay leaves, peppercorns, red chiles, tomatoes, ¼ cup of cilantro and about a tablespoon of salt. Bring to a boil and then simmer for 5 hours. Remove meat and cool. Cut into pieces roughly 2 inches square, then shred pieces by hand. Place in a 9" × 11" baking dish and cover with salad dressing. Marinate overnight.

Top beef with chopped green chiles and cheese squares. Then decorate with avocado slices and sprinkle on remaining cilantro and chopped parsley. Bake at 325° for 20 to 30 minutes, until meat is heated through.

Also may be served cold.

*Italian Dressing: 6 ounces oil, 2 ounces vinegar, salt, pepper, ½ teaspoon dried oregano, and ½ teaspoon basil.

Carne Asada — TEX-MEX Grilling

1 flank steak

Coffee Mop Sauce

½ cup tomato sauce

1 cup strong black coffee

¼ cup Worcestershire sauce

1 T. sugar

1 T. salt

1 T. pepper

1 stick butter

Combine and simmer 20 minutes and cool. Marinate the flank steak in the coffee mop sauce several hours. Grill over charcoal, generously mopping frequently. The mop sauce is also good for marinating and basting grilled beef, chicken, pork, lamb and venison.

Cabrito Asada (baby goat)

Cabrito is a popular meat for barbeques in south Texas and Mexico. Have the butcher split and clean the whole baby goat. Marinate the meat in the coffee mop sauce for 4 hours. Grill very slowly over a low fire until tender, turning and mopping frequently.

Chili   *serves 8*

2 lbs. coarse ground beef (chili grind)

2 medium onions, chopped

2 cloves garlic, crushed

2 t. cumin

6 T. or more chili powder

1 t. salt

2 16 oz. can tomatoes

¼ t. ground red pepper

1 T. sugar

Sauté onions in vegetable oil. Add the garlic, meat and seasonings and brown. Add the tomatoes, cover and simmer 2 hours.

Prepare Chili at least a day before serving. A pot of good Chili needs time to mellow.

Venison Chili   *serves 8 to 12*

3 lbs. venison, chopped or chili ground

2 lbs. lean beef, chopped or chili ground

4 T. bacon drippings (or vegetable oil)

3 large onions, chopped

2 16 oz. cans tomatoes

4 cups water

1 T. salt

1 T. pepper

5 to 6 T. chili powder

1 clove garlic

3 T. paprika

1 t. oregano

1 t. cumin

1½ t. sugar

Brown meat in fat or drippings in a large heavy pan. Add
onions and garlic, cook until golden. Add water and tomatoes; reduce heat and simmer covered for about 3 hours,
stirring occasionally. Add the seasonings and continue at
a simmer for another hour. Serve immediately or cover and
refrigerate or freeze. Makes 1 gallon.

Chorizo (Mexican Sausage)

1 lb. ground lean pork

1 t. salt

2 T. chili powder

¼ t. cumin

½ t. oregano

2 cloves garlic, pressed

2 T. vinegar

Mix all ingredients. Form into patties and fry without oil. This is best if allowed to sit overnight in the refrigerator and then made into patties.

Serve for breakfast or brunch with Huevos Rancheros. Form into meatballs and serve with hot sauce for an interesting appetizer. Better yet, use instead of seasoned beef in Chalupas Compuestas.

Chiles Verdes con Carne   *serves 6*

2 lbs. lean stew beef cut into 1 inch cubes

1 t. salt

1 to 2 cups beef stock

1 cup chopped onion

1 16 oz. can tomatoes

7(!) 4 oz. cans chopped green chiles

1 clove garlic, chopped

Brown the beef in 1 T. hot oil in a large heavy pot. Add the remaining ingredients and simmer for about 2 hours or until the beef is tender. Sometimes it is necessary to add a little more stock if the stew looks dry. Serve with or over pinto beans and/or rice.

A good make-ahead buffet supper dish. Freezes well.

Mexican Chicken

1 T. butter

1½ t. ground cumin

1 t. salt

½ t. chili powder

1 3 lb. chicken

Rub the chicken with 1 tablespoon butter. Place ½ medium onion, sliced; a rib of celery with leaves, cut in sticks; a carrot; and a few sprigs of parsley in the body cavity. Tie the legs together and sprinkle the chicken liberally with the combined spices. Place in a shallow pan in a 450° oven. After 10 minutes, reduce the heat to 325° and bake for 45 minutes or until done (the leg bone moves easily). Serve with Mexican rice and an avocado and grapefruit salad for an easy, low calorie supper.

Chicken breasts may also be cooked with these spices on a bed of the vegetables with a delicious result - reduce cooking time to 30 minutes.

Smoked Turkey stuffed with Tamales

1 15 lb. turkey

Barbeque Sauce (p. 77)

3 dozen tamales (p. 54)

Smoke the turkey in a covered heavy-duty smoker grill. Baste frequently with the sauce. Cook over low heat for 8 to 10 hours. Use charcoal with hickory or mesquite chips. Test for doneness as you would an oven-baked turkey. When the turkey is done, stuff with the warm, shucked and broken tamales. Baked at 250° for 30 minutes. Use the barbeque sauce for gravy.

Crumbled, re-cooked tamales are a delightfully different dressing — not unlike cornbread stuffing — a delicious surprise for a buffet supper!

Barbeque Sauce

1 cup ketsup

2 cups vinegar

½ cup vegetable oil

½ cup butter, melted

3 T. sugar

1 large onion, grated

4 cloves garlic, minced

¼ cup Worcestershire sauce

1 lemon, juiced

2 T. dry mustard

3 T. chili powder

2 t. salt

2 t. pepper

Combine ingredients and simmer 20 minutes.

Arroz con Pollo (Good ol' Chicken and Rice)

1 frying chicken, cut into serving pieces or 6 chicken breasts

½ cup oil

½ cup chopped onion (one small onion, chopped)

1 cup uncooked rice

¼ cup chopped green Bell pepper

1 clove garlic, minced

½ cup water

1 28 oz. can tomatoes, undrained

Juice of ½ lime

1 t. salt

½ t. cumin

1 t. chili powder

½ t. dried sweet basil or 1 T. fresh sweet basil, chopped

¼ t. oregano

In a heavy skillet, with a tight fitting cover, brown chicken lightly in the oil. Remove chicken from pan and set aside. Sauté onion and pepper until just golden brown. Remove onion and pepper with slotted spoon and set aside. Sauté the rice until golden, stirring frequently. Return onion, pepper, garlic, tomatoes, water, salt and seasonings and bring to a boil. Add the browned chicken, cover tightly and simmer for 30 minutes or until chicken is tender. This dish may also be cooked in the oven in a heavy casserole after browning steps on top of stove. Bake 45 minutes in 325° oven. Garnish with parsley and pimentos for color.

Easy to prepare ahead of time for reheating. Children love this dish!

Mexican Chicken Portuguese   *serves 12*

6 cups cooked, chopped chicken

1 lb. Velveeta cheese, cut in chunks

1 lb. Longhorn cheese, grated

1 pint sour cream

1 3 oz. jar sliced pimentos

2 10 oz. cans tomatoes and green chiles

3 medium onions, chopped

1 clove garlic, minced

1 T. oil

2 bell peppers, seeded and chopped (optional)

Cook the onion and garlic in oil until transparent. Add the tomatoes and green chiles and bring to a boil. Reduce the heat and simmer until thick, about 20 minutes. Add the cheeses and heat slowly until melted. Then add the chicken and sour cream. Heat until hot and smooth, but do not boil. Serve over a layer of rice and a layer of crisp tostado strips.

This is a great dish for a buffet supper with roast beef or ham. For luncheon serve simply with a green salad!

Chilaquiles

1 10 oz. can tomatoes with green chiles (drain and save the juice)

2 16 oz. cans tomatillos, drained

1 clove garlic, crushed

1 large onion, chopped

½ t. cumin (optional)

1½ t. salt (or to taste)

1½ to 2 cups sour cream

2 dozen tortillas

¾ lb. Monterey Jack cheese, grated

3 cups cooked chopped or shredded chicken (seasoned with some tomato liquid and ½ cup sour cream)

Make the green tomato sauce by putting the first six ingredients into a blender or food processor. Blend briefly until mixed well but still a little lumpy. Simmer in a saucepan about 30 minutes. Cool slightly and add sour cream. In a 9" × 13" pan layer stale or leftover or fresh tortillas (crisp or soft) with cheese and chicken and sauce. Save a little cheese to sprinkle over top. Bake at 325° for 30 minutes.

If you have a little leftover ham, chorizo or beef, these may also be added or substituted for the chicken. Chilaquiles in Southern Mexico is known as "old clothes." This is a dish to improvise with whatever one has. Some like to add another cup of sour cream thinned with chicken broth and tomato juice. The possibilities are endless! Prepare several hours ahead if convenient. If sour cream is too fattening, try substituting puréed cottage cheese.

Chilaquiles con Pollo   *serves 8 to 10*

1 chicken, cooked and deboned (p. 14)

2 large onions, chopped

3 cloves garlic, chopped

½ cup oil

2 10 oz. cans tomatoes and green chiles, undrained

1 16 oz. can tomatoes, undrained

1 T. cilantro (coriander)

Salt to taste

24 corn tortillas

2 lb. Monterey Jack cheese, grated

2 cups sour cream

Sauté onion and garlic in oil until transparent. Add all cans of tomatoes, cilantro, and salt. Simmer 10 to 15 minutes. Cut tortillas into fourths. In another skillet dip tortillas into the hot oil until soft (a minute or less). Drain on paper towels. In a large casserole layer tortillas, sauce, chicken, and cheese. Bake at 350° for 20 to 30 minutes or until bubbly. Serve with a dish of sour cream to the side of the casserole dish. This may be prepared in advance and refrigerated or frozen.

Chimichangas   *serves 6*

2 to 2½ lbs. stew beef

3 cloves garlic, minced

1½ t. cumin

3 T chili powder

1 onion, sliced

1 t. salt

½ t. pepper

6 8-inch flour tortillas

Place cut up stew beef and seasonings in a sauce pan. Add enough water to cover beef. Simmer covered about 2 hours or until meat is tender. Reserve broth. Shred beef when cool enough to handle. Moisten shredded beef with ½ cup of cooking broth. Add more salt and pepper, if needed.

Wrap the tortillas tightly in foil. Bake at 350° for 15 minutes. Place 3 to 4 T of beef in the tortillas . Fold the right and left sides of the tortilla to partially cover the filling. Roll the tortilla from bottom to top. Heat about 1 inch of oil in a skillet to 350°. Place the rolled tortillas seam side down in the skillet. Fry 2 or 3 at a time 1 minute per side or until golden. Serve on a bed of chopped lettuce. Top with sour cream and guacamole and pass the salsa.

Bean Burritos

Follow the same procedure as in Beef Burritos for heating the tortillas. Spread each tortilla with 3 tablespoons hot refried beans (pp. 87 & 89). Top with some or all of the following toppings: grated cheese, chopped onions, shredded lettuce, sour cream, guacamole, salsa.   Fold the right and left sides of the tortilla to partially cover the filling. Roll the tortilla from bottom to top.

Tacos Dorados — Flautas

Prepare either ground beef filling (p. 15) or the chicken filling (p. 15). Soften corn tortillas in hot oil. Place the filling in the middle of the tortilla and roll the tortilla and secure the flap with a tooth pick. Place ½ inch of oil in a skillet, heat over medium heat and fry until golden and crisp (about 2 minutes). Drain these well, tilting slightly so the oil runs out. Remove toothpick or at least warn your guests. Serve the Tacos Dorados on a bed of shredded lettuce, topped with a generous helping of guacamole and sour cream. Sprinkle with chopped onion.

Beef Burritos   *serves 12*

1 recipe Chiles Verdes con Carne (p. 75)

1 medium onion, minced

2 cups Monterey Jack or Longhorn cheese, grated

12   8-inch flour tortillas

Tightly wrap the tortillas in foil. Heat in 350° oven for 15 minutes. Using a slotted spoon, place the meat filling in the tortilla. Sprinkle with onion and cheese. Fold the right and left sides of the tortilla to partially cover the filling. Roll the tortilla from bottom to top, and serve immediately. These are quick, and everyone can make their own if you like.

VEGETABLES

Texican Squash *serves 8 to 10*

2½ lbs. summer squash (yellow, zucchini, pattypan), cubed or sliced

4 eggs

½ cup milk

1 lb. Monterey Jack cheese, cubed or grated

1 t. salt

2 t. baking powder

3 T. flour

½ cup chopped parsley

1 4 oz. can chopped green chiles

2 chopped, seeded jalapeños (optional)

1½ cups crushed tostados or bread crumbs

Cook squash in 2 cups water until barely tender, about 7 minutes at a boil. Drain and cool in collander. Mix eggs, milk, cheese, salt, baking powder, flour, parsley, and chiles together. Fold into squash. Butter an oblong pyrex 3 quart dish, 9″ by 13″. Sprinkle bottom with crushed tostado crumbs, or bread crumbs if you prefer. Pour in squash mixture. Sprinkle top with more crumbs. Bake at 350° for 30 minutes.

Corn and Squash Mexican   *serves 8 to 10*

2 lbs. summer squash, zucchini and yellow crookneck is an attractive combination

1 large onion, chopped

4 ears fresh, sweet corn

4 T. butter

1 cup grated Monterey Jack cheese

1 or 2 jalapeños, finely chopped

Cook squash in 1 cup water until tender 10 to 15 minutes. Drain in collander. Sauté onion in butter. Cut corn from cob. Combine squash, onion, corn, jalapeños and cheese. Pour into casserole. Bake at 325° for about 30 minutes.

Squash and Hominy Dish   *serves 8 to 10*

2 lbs. yellow squash or zucchini

2 cans drained hominy

½ lb. sharp cheese, grated

2 or more jalapeño peppers, seeded and chopped

1½ cups sour cream

1 t. salt

1 large onion, chopped

½ stick butter

Cook the squash, onion and butter slowly until tender with ½ cup water in skillet. Add the remaining ingredients, reserving 1 cup of cheese. Pour into a 3 quart casserole and top with the remaining cheese. Sprinkle with leftover crushed tostados or Doritos. Bake at 325° for 1 hour.

Green Chile Hominy Casserole   *serves 8*

2 20 oz. cans white hominy

2 4 oz. cans chopped green chiles

2 cups sour cream

2 cups Monterey Jack cheese, grated

1 cup half & half cream

4 oz. butter

salt & pepper

Drain hominy. Layer half a can of hominy in bottom of a 3 quart casserole. Add ½ cup sour cream, ½ cup cheese and a half can of green chiles. Dot each layer of hominy with butter and sprinkle with salt and pepper. Repeat layers and end with cheese. Just before baking pour the cream over the casserole to prevent drying out. Bake at 350° for 40 to 50 minutes.

Pinto Beans, Frijoles   *serves 8 to 10*

1 lb. package dried pinto beans

1 large onion, chopped

1 10 oz. can tomatoes and green chiles

1 T. salt

1 T. sugar

2 T. chili powder

½ lb. of bacon (cut into small pieces and sautéed)

Wash the beans and pick out rocks. Place in a 2 quart pan and cover beans with 4 cups of water. Soak for a few hours if time permits. Bring to a boil, lower heat, add the other ingredients. Simmer for 4 hours, adding water when needed to keep beans just covered with liquid, stirring occasionally until the beans are soft and the juice is thick.

Borracho Beans   *serves 8*

2 cups dried pinto beans

1 clove garlic, crushed

Salt pork

2 T. bacon drippings

1 onion, chopped

2 jalapeño peppers

2 tomatoes (or one 16 oz. can drained)

1 can beer

Soak beans in water overnight. Drain and cover with fresh water. Add 2 teaspoons salt, garlic and pork. Simmer 2½ hours or until beans are soft. Drain beans and reserve liquid. Heat bacon drippings and sauté the onions, peppers and tomatoes until soft. Stir the mixture into beans and simmer 5 minutes. Just before serving, pour beer and as much reserved liquid as desired into beans. Serve hot. Beans can be mashed or "processed" for refrieds.

Black Beans   *serves 8 to 10*

1 lb. package of black turtle beans

6 cups water

1 medium onion

1 large clove of garlic

1 bay leaf

3 slices of bacon or 3 oz. salt pork, diced

2 seeded jalapeño peppers (medium size)

Salt and pepper to taste

Rinse and carefully look through the beans for pebbles.

Combine all the ingredients in a 3 quart sauce pan. Bring to a boil and simmer covered for 3 hours or until tender.

Stir from time to time to be sure beans do not stick and scorch. Add water to keep beans just covered with liquid.

Refried Beans, Frijoles Refritas

½ to 1 cup vegetable oil, lard or bacon drippings

1 recipe of pinto beans or black beans

Heat the oil over medium heat in a skillet or electric fry pan. Add a ¼ of the beans at a time and mash with a potato masher by hand. Continue to mash and stir until the oil has been absorbed and the beans are shiny in appearance (about 30 minutes). Don't overcook or they become too dry. Place these in a casserole dish, top with grated Monterey Jack cheese. Serve immediately or reheat in a 325° oven for 15 to 20 minutes when needed.

Mexican Rice   *serves 6 to 8*

1 cup uncooked rice

½ cup bacon drippings

½ cup chopped onion

1 clove garlic, minced

½ cup chopped green pepper (optional)

3 cups canned tomatoes or V-8 juice or a combination of fresh tomatoes and beef broth

Salt

Sauté the rice, onions, garlic and green pepper in the bacon drippings until the rice is golden. Then add tomatoes or tomato juice to the rice. Cover and simmer for 30 minutes. If the rice begins to appear too dry, add a little water.

A standard accompaniment for any Mexican meal.

BREADS

Flour Tortillas

2 cups flour

½ t. salt

4 T. lard or shortening

½ cup hot water

Mix salt into flour. Cut lard or shortening into flour until uniform crumbly texture is reached. Add hot water gradually, mixing with a fork until dough forms a ball. Knead with your hands on a floured board until dough is elastic and smooth — about 5 minutes. Cover and let dough rest for 10 minutes. Divide dough into 12 golf-ball-sized balls. Roll out one at a time on floured board until approximately 7 inches in diameter. Cook on a hot ungreased griddle 20 to 30 seconds on each side — until spotted and tender. Serve immediately with butter or keep warm in a folded dish towel for up to an hour until serving time. These flour tortillas are so easy and so good — another children's favorite. Flour tortillas may be used for Soft Tacos (p. 53), in Chilaquiles (p. 80) and even in making enchiladas. Corn tortillas are generally used in this cookbook's recipes, unless otherwise specified.

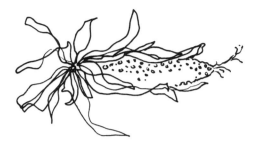

Jalapeño Corn Bread   *serves 10 to 12*

1½ cups yellow cornmeal

3 t. baking powder

½ t. salt

1 cup grated Longhorn cheese

1 cup grated onions

5 large jalapeños, finely chopped

3 eggs, lightly beaten

½ cup corn oil

1 cup sour cream

1 8½ oz. can cream style corn or 3 ears fresh corn, cut and scraped from cob

Mix together cornmeal, baking powder and salt. Stir in cheese, onions and jalapeños. Add eggs, oil, sour cream and corn; mix well. Grease a 9″ by 13″ pan and pour in the batter. Bake at 400° for 20 to 30 minutes or until a straw comes out clean.

Bake Jalapeño Corn Bread batter in greased miniature muffin tins, and cook only 10 to 15 minutes in a 400° oven. Attractive luncheon muffins or appetizers!

Sopaipillas   *3 dozen*

4 cups flour

1 T. shortening

1 t. salt

4 t. baking powder

1 beaten egg

1 cup water

Sift flour, baking powder and salt. Mix in shortening and knead. Add egg and water to form a stiff dough. Divide dough into four parts and roll out very thin. Then cut into 3 inch squares. Fry in deep hot fat — 350°. The sopaipillas puff up like little pillows! Serve immediately with honey.

DESSERTS

Flan

6 eggs, lightly beaten

½ cup plus 1 T. sugar

1 t. vanilla

½ t. salt

3 cups milk

½ cup sugar

1 T. water

1 T. rum

Combine the first five ingredients in a food processor and blend until smooth. Place ½ cup sugar, water and rum in a skillet over medium heat. Stir continually until syrupy and brown; pour into lightly greased 7½" by 11", 2 quart baking dish. Add the custard. Place the dish in a hot water bath and bake at 325° for one hour or until knife inserted in custard comes out clean. Allow an additional 30-45 minutes baking time if you use a deep flan dish.

Pralines I

2 cups sugar

1 cup brown sugar

1 stick butter

1 cup evaporated milk

2 T. light corn syrup

4 cups pecan halves

Place all the ingredients except the pecans in a heavy pan. Heat over medium high heat, stirring, until the mixture boils. Continue boiling over low heat until the soft ball stage, 238°, on a candy thermometor is reached (about 30 minutes). Remove from heat. Beat until creamy and beginning to thicken. Add the pecans and drop by spoonfuls on wax paper. Cool. Store in air tight containers.

Pralines II

2 lbs. light brown sugar

2 cups granulated white sugar

¾ cup light corn syrup

1 cup milk

3 t. vanilla

½ stick, 2 ozs., butter

1 lb. pecan halves or pieces

Cook brown and white sugars, corn syrup and milk to soft ball stage, 240°, without stirring. Remove from heat and add vanilla and butter. Beat by hand until the mixture thickens and drops easily from a spoon. Add the nuts. Drop mixture, a generous tablespoon at a time, onto the waxed paper. Candy will set and harden quickly. If mixture hardens in the pan, add a very small amount of hot water and stir until it softens. Cool and store in an air tight container.

Bananas

6 slightly green bananas, peeled and halved lengthwise

½ cup brown sugar

⅓ cup butter

cinnamon

½ cup rum

¼ cup liqueur, brandy, Grand Marnier, etc.

Melt the butter and sugar in a shallow sauté pan. Sauté the cinnamon sprinkled bananas 1 minute on each side. Pour in the rum and liqueur, ignite. If you do not wish to flame, use only ¼ cup rum. Serve immediately with ice cream or/and whipped cream — Scoop up pan juices to pour over all.

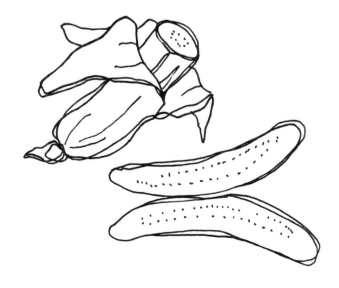

Three Fruit Ice

1¼ cups sugar

1¼ cups water

2 t. unflavored gelatin

¼ cup cold water

1 cup lemon juice

1 cup orange juice

5 bananas, peeled and well mashed

2 egg whites, stiffly beaten

Soften gelatin in the cold water. Boil 1¼ cups water and sugar together for 5 minutes. Add softened gelatin to the hot syrup. Cool to room temperature and add lemon juice, orange juice and bananas. Chill in refrigerator. Add stiffly beaten egg whites and freeze in ice trays or in an ice cream freezer — hand cranked is best!

So refreshing after a big Mexican meal.

Oranges With Wine Sauce

2 cups dry red wine

½ cup sugar

1½ cups boiling water

12 cloves

2 sticks cinnamon

1 T. raisins or currants

1 tangerine, sliced and unpeeled

12 navel oranges

In a pyrex or enamel saucepan, dissolve sugar in the water and add the wine. Add cloves, cinnamon, raisins, tangerine and lemon to the wine mixture and boil slowly until the liquid becomes syrupy, about 35 to 40 minutes. Strain out the spices and fruit with a sieve or slotted spoon. Peel the oranges with a sharp knife removing all the white membrane. Remove segments. Add the orange segments to the wine sauce and chill. Serve garnished with sliced almonds and finely slivered orange peel.

In winter, serve the sauce piping hot with the oranges — so fragrant! For a summer treat use this sauce with fresh, juicy, sliced peaches or pears instead of oranges. Prepare wine sauce ahead and use as needed — keeps weeks refrigerated.

Fresh Mangoes

Chilled, ripe, fresh mangoes with a slice of lime makes a delightful dessert after a heavy meal.

Mexican Custard Sauce

2 cups whole milk

6 eggs yolks

⅓ cup sugar

¼ t. salt

1 T. vanilla

1 cup whipping cream

1 to 2 T. rum (or tequila!)

Beat egg yolks with sugar and salt. Heat milk but do not boil. Add gradually to the egg yolk mixture. Cook in double boiler over boiling water until custard will coat a spoon. Add vanilla and chill in refrigerator. Whip cream. When ready to serve, fold rum and whipped cream into custard and serve over fresh fruit: oranges, berries, peaches – cake, brownies, mango mousse.

Vanilla and chocolate are native to Mexico.

INDEX

IT'S A LONG WAY TO GUACAMOLE
*The **TEX-MEX** Cookbook*

P.O. Box 983
Arlington, VA 22216
703/538-2393

Please send me _____ copies of
    It's a Long Way to Guacamole   @ $10.95 each _____
Postage and handling   @   2.25 each _____
    Virginia residents, add $ .49 sales tax   _____
                                       Total _____

Name _____

Address _____

City _____ State _____ Zip _____

Phone _____

    Enclose Check/Money Order payable to *J & W Tex-Mex.*

IT'S A LONG WAY TO GUACAMOLE
*The **TEX-MEX** Cookbook*

P.O. Box 983
Arlington, VA 22216
703/538-2393

Please send me _____ copies of
It's a Long Way to Guacamole   @ $10.95 each _____
Postage and handling   @   2.25 each _____
    Virginia residents, add $ .49 sales tax   _____
                                         Total _____

Name _____

Address _____

City _____ State _____ Zip _____

Phone _____

    Enclose Check/Money Order payable to *J & W Tex Mex.*